M000105341

83 THINGS I WISH THE BLACK CHURCH WOULD STOP DOING

MILAN FORD

published by

ThePewView.com

83 Things I Wish The Black Church Would Stop Doing
Copyright © 2009 By Milan Ford
Published By ThePewView.com

ISBN-13: 978-0-692-00677-1
ISBN: 069200677X

All rights reserved. No part of this book may be reproduced or transmitted in any form of by any means, electronic or mechanical, including photocopying and recording, or by any information storage and retrieval system, without permission in writing from the publisher.

Published in the United States of America

Cover Design: Milan Ford
Interior Design & Layout: Milan Ford
Interior Photography & Illustration: iStockphoto.com
Editor: Lisa Birch

All Scripture quotations, unless otherwise indicated, are taken from the Holy Bible, New King James Translation.

Copyright © 1982 by Thomas Nelson Inc.
Used by permission. All rights reserved.

you cannot change what you
have not first learned to love.

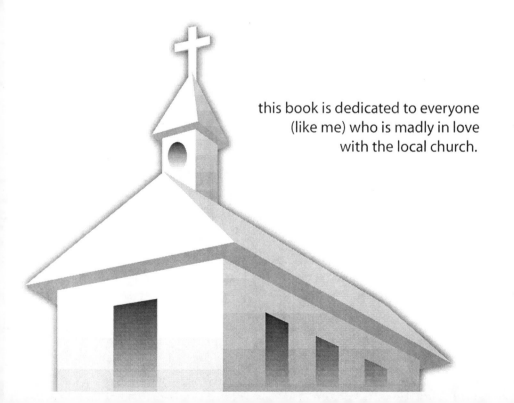

this book is dedicated to everyone
(like me) who is madly in love
with the local church.

contents

why 83?   8

commercial break:

why 83?

Well, I have a rather short answer to that.

As well as a long answer.

I'll knock out the longer of the two first.

On Monday, April 28, 2008,
while sitting on my couch at home,
I had the opportunity to watch **Rev. Jeremiah Wright,**
former pastor of The United Church of Christ, located
in Chicago, Illinois, speak to the National Press Club
in Washington, D.C. on matters of faith and race.

Now just in case you may have been living
on planet Mars around that time, Rev. Wright was
caught in a media firestorm concerning some
video snippets of a series of messages he had once
preached regarding God's judgment of America.

The video snippets grabbed national headlines arguably
not for its volatile content, but primarily because

President Barack Obama,

along with his wife, First Lady Michelle Obama,
and their two children, Sasha and Malia,
were all members of Wright's congregation;
President Obama for nearly 20 years.

In an effort to unveil whether or not President Obama,
then just Senator Obama, who was at that time
picking up speed on the campaign trail, was in fact
someone who endorsed and supported the kind of
messages Rev. Wright was preaching, one of the most
demonizing media campaigns I had ever witnessed
involving a spiritual leader (black or white) began.

Rev. Jeremiah Wright, a man who had led his church
congregation for over 36 years, served for 2 years
as a private first class in the 2nd Marine Division,
who prior to entering college and seminary school,
trained as a cardio pulmonary technician at the
Naval Medical Center, located in Bethesda, Maryland.

The same center that in which Wright was personally responsible for helping President Lyndon B. Johnson recover from heart surgery back in 1966.

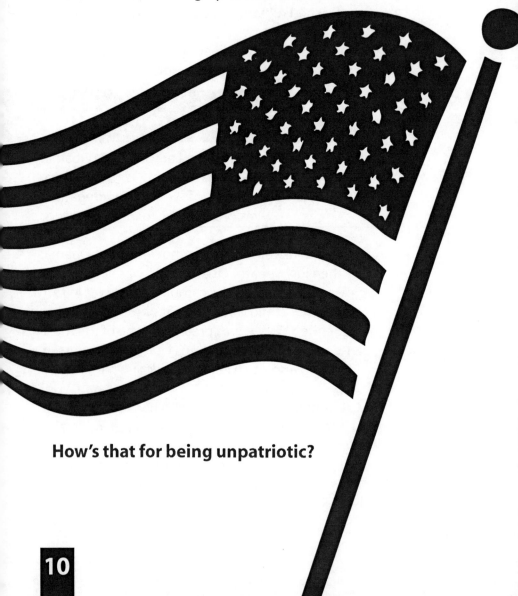

How's that for being unpatriotic?

Yet despite his years of service, on Monday, April 28, 2008, I watched as Rev. Jeremiah Wright approached the podium at the National Press Club, of what I just knew would serve as a total reversal of fortune; a complete and necessary vindication for a man who was arguably one of the most influential African-American ministry leaders of his generation.

But what I heard (and saw) on that day…
…well, let's just say I've never been the same since.

Rev. Wright discussed how the uproar from his messages was in large part a direct result of those who have yet to understand the historical and philosophical ideologies of the **'black church.'**

Wright firmly believed that the recent attack on him was not solely based on the pursuit of conservative media and politicians to derail Obama from winning the presidency, but that it was also an attack on the **'black church'** as a whole.

I'll never forget one particular statement he made on that day; a statement that while I wholeheartedly agreed with him at the time, caused me to cringe in my seat as he said it.

"We (the black church) are not deficient, we're just different."

After hearing his defense, and rather colorful exchanges with the National Press Club moderator, I leaned over to my wife, who sat beside me that day to watch the interview, and whispered these words to her:

"This is going to change everything."

Some how, some way, something within me knew that
for the weeks and months that would follow that
interview, one that was played over and over again on
every major cable news network I could turn to,
no other phrase would be the topic of discussion
than that of the **'black church.'**

And sadly, I was right.

I can't even begin to tell you how many editorials,
blogs, and open forums I remember reading later that
summer from pastors, theologians and civic leaders alike
who, like Wright, passionately believed that the **'black church'**
or 'black worship' experience was different than any other.

Not deficient.
Just different.

As a 33 year old ministry leader, who has spent 31 of those
years growing and maturing within two predominately
African-American churches, that was a belief
I once held as well.

From its unique form of musical expression,
oratorical patterns of delivering the word of God,
as well as its ability to provide a 'liberating' method of
evangelism to the surrounding community,
I firmly believed that the **'black church'** was something
that would surely stand the test of time.

That was until the fall of 2002.

After serving as a student leader for nearly 3 ½ years within the college ministry of a church I was attending at the time, I was given the opportunity to become the ministry's director.

The church was (and still is) one of the largest and most influential congregations in the country, led by an awesome pastor and visionary, who possessed an immeasurable passion to reach the hearts and minds of this generation, specifically of (late) Busters and Mosaics; those who were born between the years of 1974 and 2002.

For nearly 4 years, I had the opportunity to serve, counsel, lead, and learn from hundreds of college students, most of whom attended historically black colleges and universities.

And during that span of time, I witnessed first hand what many ministry leaders within churches all across this country are experiencing today; a growing **discontentment** and apathy regarding the relevance of the local church in the eyes of today's generation of young people.

Despite all of the programs, events, concerts, scholarships, pizza nights, and other heart felt approaches our churches have tried to offer in order to reach this generation, what was once considered necessary, has now become optional.

And worse, what was once attractive…**now repels.**

Statistics continue to show that many college-aged students (between the ages of 18-25) who regularly attended church while in high school, **stop attending church** altogether within two years of their college graduation.

(be sure to pick up a copy of Dave Kinnaman and Gabe Lyon's book, unChristian: What A New Generation Really Thinks About Christianity. Required reading in my opinion)

While many would like to attribute this decline in church attendance among 18-25 year olds as the result of a corrupt, new age, materialistic, and media saturated culture that is opposed to anything that looks like God…

…I now have a **different** opinion.

One that was formed when running across this interesting passage of scripture late one night:

Mark 7:1-8,13 (NKJV)

Then the Pharisees and some of the scribes came together to Him, having come from Jerusalem.

Now when they saw some of His disciples eat bread with defiled, that is with unwashed hands, they found fault.

*For the Pharisees and all the Jews do not eat unless they wash their hands in a special way, holding the **tradition** of the elders.*

When they come from the marketplace, they do not eat unless they wash.

And there are many other things which they have received and hold, like the washing of cups, pitchers, copper vessels, and couches.

*Then the Pharisees and scribes asked Him, "Why do Your disciples not walk according to **the tradition of the elders,** but eat bread with unwashed hands?"*

He answered and said to them, "Well did Isaiah prophesy of you hypocrites, as it is written:

'This people honors Me with their lips, but their heart is far from Me. And in vain they worship Me, teaching as doctrines the commandments of men.'

*For laying aside the commandment of God, **you hold the tradition of men...***

*...making the word of God of no effect through your **tradition** which you handed down.*

And many such things you do.

As we see here in this passage,
Jesus made it painfully clear.

Nothing can nullify and cause our efforts
to reach this generation appear to be fruitless
in the sight of God more than some of the **traditions**
found within the local church.

Even those traditions that we have long stood
by as 'different,' may in fact be more 'deficient' and
unproductive than many of us care to realize.

In 2008, I was provided with the opportunity to
serve as a 'content editor' for the world's largest
provider of online broadcasting services to the
faith-based community.

From the streaming of live worship services,
to the creation of social media integrated strategies
the local church can use to effectively communicate
the gospel, this company does it all.

What I found interesting however is that over **85%**
of this company's clientele consists of predominately
African-American churches or ministries.

In fact, if I were a betting man, it would not surprise
me if after I assembled all of the cable television
networks in the world that currently broadcast
faith-based programming…

…I'd discover that over **60%** of their content
would be produced by or at least targeted to reach
predominately African-American believers.

**And why is that important
to point out, you ask?**

Thanks to the American phenomenon of televangelism, and those networks and companies that seek to capitalize on the commercial appeal of faith and religion, many of the traditions and charismatic practices found within the **'black church'** can be seen all around the world.

Today, the style of the **'black church'** is often more celebrated than the substance it seeks to provide.

Take a stroll through your local college campus community on any day of the week, or turn on the radio to your city's favorite R&B or Hip-Hop station, and you'll soon discover that the practices of the **'black church'** are often the butt of every religious joke today offered by this generation.

It is undeniable that our traditions and practices have become much louder than the message of Christ we seek to deliver.

So how in the world can this problem be adequately addressed?

*How can I convince a cell phone company that our churches are worth more than just **the sound** our choirs make?*

*How can I persuade some of the largest ministry leadership conferences in the world that have yet to include any African-American pastors as keynote speakers, that many of them are able to speak in a relevant manner without **breaking into song?***

*And how can I stamp out once and for all the belief that a large majority of our youth and young adults have today that all the local church wants from them is **their money?***

Pretty big task isn't it?

17

But one Saturday afternoon, it came to me.

As I was watching arguably the greatest gift God ever gave the family-trying-to-save-on-some-bills-so-they-decided-to-finally-cut-all-the-premium-channels-off, Turner Network Television (TNT)...

...the movie **Eight Mile** came on.

Eight Mile, featuring none other than hip-hop rapper Eminem, Brittany Murphy, and Kim Basinger, wasn't exactly a favorite of mine.

Although I had seen the movie before, I was slightly curious as to how TNT was going to pull this one off.

Nothing cracks me up more than watching some of Hollywood's most memorable movies re-edited with voiceovers and at times, special effects, in order to eliminate any obscenities unsuitable for primetime viewership.

Trust me; they butchered Coming To America!

For those who haven't seen Eight Mile, there is a scene at the very end of the movie where Eminem's character (Rabbit) is participating in a freestyle rap battle with other notable rappers inside the infamous Detroit night club, The Shelter.

Rabbit, who has had his share of bad experiences in rap battles before, has finally mustered up enough confidence to showcase the skills he and his friends always knew he had.

When battling the first two contestants he faced, the crowd (responsible for all the judging) declared Rabbit as the winner.

But then came round three.

It was time for Rabbit to now face the reigning champion of the rap battle, Papa Doc--someone Rabbit knew personally and had a number of physical altercations with.

After being warned by his friends that Papa Doc may win the battle on the count that he could use everything he already knew personally about Rabbit against him...

The fact that Rabbit was white.
Or that he lived in a trailer park.
Or perhaps that he had probably the most unintelligent
bunch of friends in the entire city of Detroit.

...Rabbit came up with a brilliant plan.

Something very few churches and ministry leaders have the courage to do today.

He decided to go **FIRST.**

By going first I mean he decided to disarm Papa Doc by exposing and disdaining everything he already knew was a target point for ridicule, leaving nothing else left to talk about.

This risky move made by Rabbit to deal with the negative, and to do so FIRST, paid off.

Papa Doc was left speechless.
A cardinal sin in any rap battle.

So, after all of the rambling I've done so far, what is this book really all about?

It's about going FIRST.

It's about taking the time to examine how some of the things we do in church appear in the eyes of today's generation.

But I believe it's my duty to warn you:

This book may make some of you **LAUGH.**
This book may make some of you **THINK.**
This book may even make some of you **ANGRY.**

But most importantly, it is my prayer that this book will ignite a passion inside the heart of every local church to do whatever it has to in order to win this generation for the cause of Christ.

Even if it means making a little fun of itself.

'Cause let's face it;
no one takes themselves
more seriously than Christians.

Perhaps if we can humble ourselves, and admit
where we are in need of some **correction**
and adjustment as the local church...

...then maybe the awesome power and glory
of our God can finally be lifted back up
where it should be. (See John 12:32)

So there you have it.

That's my long answer for why there are
83 Things I Wish The Black Church Would Stop Doing.

And as for the shorter answer:

I just figured 83 was a good place to stop.

The Assigned Reader

I can think of only one moment in history when this kind of exchange was even remotely interesting.

Pong.
The classic Atari video game.

Reading may indeed be fundamental, but when a pastor selects someone to read a passage of scripture aloud, even though he or she plans to come right behind them to read it again…

…well, that's just (fundamentally) weird.

Sometimes keeping the ball in play for too long can be a huge waste of time.

And like Pong, the longer you do, the more difficult it may be for you to score.

And win.

23

The Contracted Musician

Never understood how this works.

To contract a musician to play on 1st and
3rd Sundays, while permitting him or her to
play at another church across town on
2nd and 4th Sundays...

...just seems like an accident waiting to happen.

I wonder what my wife would do if I told her that
I wanted to "play with" her twice a month,
as long as I can continue to "play with"
another woman across town?

She'd probably make Lorena Bobbitt
look like a girl scout.

Think the analogy is a bit far fetched, do you?

Well, just wait till it's time for some of
those contracts to be renewed.

Better to hire a member who happens to
be a musician, than to contract a musician who
has yet to value becoming a member.

Money has a way of confusing the two.

Church License Plates

Greenville, SC

Branded merchandising seems to be extremely important to any thriving church these days.

Bags.
T-Shirts.
Hats.
Coffee Mugs.

I actually know of one church who sold golf balls with their name on them.

I guess if you can reach folk on the driving range, you can just about reach anybody.

There is however one product I really wish some churches would stop branding themselves on.

License Plates.

Just think if a few of your members ever felt like showing off a little road rage on Monday morning, it may not be a good thing to let your local law enforcement see where they go to church.

Back Door Fear

No matter where you go, it seems like
everyone these days is afraid of
people leaving their church.

Some more than others.

Instead of concentrating all of our efforts
on closing the **back door** in our churches…

…maybe we should focus on opening **the front.**

When we refrain from teaching our members
how and when to (properly) leave, we often
endanger them (and our churches)
of becoming lakes.

Instead of rivers.

Ran a Wikipedia search the other day on
the difference between a lake and a river.

Here's what I found:

A river is a body of water
that runs continuously.

A lake (on the other hand) is a body of water
that lies still.

A river (I also discovered) is where water
is spent.

While a lake is where water
is stored.

And lastly, a river (for the most part)
is naturally composed.

But a lake is (more often than not)
typically man-made.

Here's a question to consider:

Which of the following do we want
our churches to be known as the most?

Naturally composed or man-made?

Sidenote: Do you know what a lake can become
if enough sediment builds up inside of it?

A swamp.

THE *Red* CARPET

**Reserved pulpit seating.
Being asked to sing a song.
Altar calls (catered only to try to reach them).**

I wonder how many celebrities and notable
business leaders would begin attending one of
our churches if we could just keep **The Red Carpet**
treatment down to a minimal.

I'm sure we all can agree that going to
the bathroom by yourself is something
anyone (famous or not) can appreciate.

Services Before 9am

When adding services, try going clockwise.
Not counter-clockwise.

Ever tried waking up a sleepy congregation
with sleepy volunteers? Pretty difficult task, isn't it?

Remember: Presentation is everything.
And so is timing.

So if you're worried about keeping those folks
who just love **'getting out'** early...

...believe me, you've lost them already.

*If you must go counter-clockwise, take a look at
stretching back to Saturday evenings.*

Could be a great strategy.

Car Washes.

Teaching our young people the value of entrepreneurship is indeed important.

But when they have to apply nearly four coats of

SPF 30

just to learn the lesson, then maybe it's time to take another look at some of our **church youth ministry budgets.**

Besides, after that water bill comes in, you may be slightly tempted to ask the kids for a little of that money back.

33

Church Staff Tenure

In 1807, Thomas Jefferson wrote these words:

"If some termination to the services of the chief Magistrate be not fixed by the Constitution, or supplied by practice, his office, nominally four years, will in fact become for life."

Shortly after FDR passed away, the only president to be elected for more than two terms, Congress passed the now infamous **Twenty-Second Amendment,** which states that no one could be elected to the office of the President more than twice.

Their reason: **Balance of power.**

I always found that interesting considering that neither the state senators nor representatives that make up Congress, have a limit as to how many terms they can be elected to serve.

Not too sure if you can call that a 'balance of power.'

I've often wondered whether or not something similar should be adopted for churches as it relates to their 'tenured' staff.

Not because of any fear of imbalanced power. But rather because of a slight fear of irrelevance.

Or worst: **Burnout.**

Imagine what it would be like if churches limited their staff members to only work for them for three-year terms, after which providing them with one of the following options:

1. Six months paid vacation.
2. One year internship at another church **out of state.**
or...
3. To return as a part-time staff member
(if and only if he or she is currently enrolled in graduate school.)

Imagine the possibilities.

I'm sure Jefferson would be proud. Congress on the other hand, may not be.

GREEN

SPACE

Unless you feel your congregation needs
a little more oxygen these days...

...let's try **toning down** all the pulpit plants.

And to my good friend, Al Gore:
Please don't be mad at me.

Full Ministry Listings

Made a startling discovery earlier this year.

While cleaning out the garage, I noticed that I had
three copies of The Yellow Pages. All wrapped in plastic bags.

The same bags they were in when they were first delivered.
Thick. Heavy. And most importantly, unused.

Once I mustered enough strength to lift them all up,
I did what any Google lover would do: **I threw them away.**

Listing all of your church ministries on your website or bulletin
is not necessary. In fact, it is quite counterproductive.

People search out what interests them most about your church.
And believe it or not, most are looking for the same things.

Take time to research and find out what those are.
And list those only.

Most of your site visitors only stay on your site for 30-45 seconds
before deciding to stay on or leave completely. Purge your listing
to showcase what is **thriving,** versus just surviving.

Besides, the **Mother's Board Clarinet Ministry** is not getting that
many site hits these days. May hurt to tell them, but somebody's got to.

Praise Countdowns

"60 seconds till…"
"For the next 30 seconds…"
"Only 10 more seconds left till…"
"Okay. You've only got 30 more seconds…"

Huh?

Although disputed by every mathematician
I have asked, I am convinced our churches
have found a way to bend time.

We have learned how to make it slow down, stand still,
and at times, even make it move backwards.

How you ask?

PDL(s): **Praise Decibel Levels**

The lower the PDL,
the slower the clock.

HELLO!
My name is...

Visitor Identification

Do you remember your very
first day at a new school?

Pretty scary day, wasn't it?

Were you at all (like me) a little nervous about whether or not you had the right kind of clothes to wear?

Or whether you'd be able to find all of your classrooms?

Did you have to find out on your own which lunch tables were off-limits to underclassmen?

Or perhaps you (like me) spent most of the day trying to find out where your locker was.

Not to mention trying to remember the locker combination.

Let's face it:
Being new is awkward.

Especially when it comes to visiting a new church for the first time. I know there are some churches that pride themselves on identifying visitors, but I'd like to make a slight suggestion:

Don't identify them.

Give them some air. Allow them to walk around freely without the big balloon and the "Hello, I Am A Visitor" name badge.

Create a welcome kiosk in your lobby for visitors to discover more about your church. At their own pace.

Doing so will help insure your church 'membership' consists of people who are not only attracted to your church, but of people who also have taken a **personal initiative** to become more involved in it.

It's perfectly okay to appreciate visitors. Just be sure to always examine the approaches you take to do so.

Nothing like talking to the new girl in school, only to find out she is already heavily involved with another boyfriend.

Took me quite a while to get over that rejection.

Predated Healing Services

I believe wholeheartedly in the healing power of our God.

However, I've also come to discover that God's healing calendar and that of our own tend to be hard to **synchronize.**

Instead of hosting weekly or monthly healing services, why not try leaving the calendar open?

Nothing like when God pays you a surprise visit.

Singles Ministry

I've always wondered why most singles ministries in our churches are led…**by singles?**

Could open the door for some tragic mishaps.

*If you insist on creating a singles ministry for your church, please promise me you'll do one of the following:

1. Locate a mature **married couple** (who has a heart for singles) to lead it.

Experience (and a ring) is always best.

And…

2. Be sure the ministry involves more than just a highlighted route to the altar.

Believe it or not, there are some singles in your church who are **NOT** consumed with finding someone to get married to.

Those empty seats at your last mixer are probably a good indication of just that.

RESERVED

church ↳ **STAFF PARKING**

PERMIT REQUIRED

VIOLATORS SUBJECT T

TICKETING & TOWING

44

After being around the church for most of my life,
I have yet to understand why we have
reserved parking spaces for people who come
nearly two hours earlier to church than anyone else.

A mystery indeed.

Membership

Jesus, I'll take your camel and raise you one elephant.

For it has become far easier for an elephant to go through the eye of a needle, than for someone to actually become a member within one of our churches today.

Honestly, some of our **'new member orientations'** would make the training necessary to become a Navy Seal look like child's play.

Isn't it interesting that when Jesus began selecting his 12 disciples, there was no orientation seminar required of them.

Their only requirement was to follow.

While today, our churches seek to require others to **BELIEVE** before they **BELONG,** Jesus did exactly the opposite.

He allowed others to **BELONG** before they (fully) **BELIEVED.**

Now more than ever before, our churches must begin to refocus our attention away from membership, and more on participation.

Membership no longer has its privileges. In fact, it has far more limitations.

Instead of reporting membership, report **PARTICIPATION.**

Besides, once you eliminate all of those names off the roster who haven't shown up to church in over 9 years, you may just realize how important your non-members really are.

The Yellow Cake

No, I'm not talking about that Nigerian uranium
our government said they found in Iraq.

No. This kind of 'yellow cake' is far more dangerous.
A real weapon of mass destruction.

I understand refreshments are still very much a
mainstay in many of our churches, especially after a
fall revival or ministry conference, but I think
it's time to consider providing a *different kind* of dessert.

Despite the fact that one slice of yellow cake can equate
to almost **425 calories** (one-fifth of our recommended
daily calorie intake), it amazes me that after spending
nearly four weeks in the church refrigerator…

…*we still dare to serve it to the kids in the children's ministry.*

I remember it like it was yesterday.

I invited a friend to church one particular Sunday; a day that (little did I know) we were scheduled to have a visiting guest psalmist sing along with our church choir.

During the A selection, all went well. Then came the B selection.

The visiting guest psalmist began to express herself through song in a **vocal artistic pattern** many have come to admire, yet one my friend had never heard before.

After the song ended, my friend leaned over to me and whispered five words I will never forget:

"Was all that really necessary?"

Remember: A ministry **TALENT** is not always considered by some as a ministry **TOOL.**

SQUALLING

THE COLOR PURPLE

In the realm of cinema,
it's one of the best.

In the realm of **church décor,**
it's one of the worst.

Okay, maybe not the worst.
Just over used.

Why not try mixing our color choices up just a bit?

Purple carpet.
Purple chairs.
Purple robes.
Purple logos.

Keep that up and we can be sure Miss Celie won't
be the only one around here with the blues.

Weekly Altar Calls

For those who are accepting God's gift of salvation for the first time, **the altar** is indeed an incredible point of transition.

No doubt about it.

But when it comes to areas of faith outside of salvation, the altar for many has become a point of **repetition.**

In a set of experiments that spanned ten years (1890-1900), **Ivan Pavlov** made a startling discovery regarding the cognitive learning habits and behavior of dogs.

If you happened to stay awake in your college Psych class (I barely did), you may remember hearing about this experiment.

Pavlov attached a device to a dog in order to measure the amount that dog would salivate when hungry.

Pavlov then would ring a bell or tone every time he gave the dog food. He did this several times.

Ring The Bell.
Feed The Dog.
Ring The Bell.
Feed The Dog.

Pavlov repeated this sequence until he notices that the dog would eventually salivate at the sound of the bell.

Whether there was food available or not.

Believe it or not, this kind of automatic, non-conscious learning is not only present in dogs and other animals, but it is present in us as humans as well.

At the sight of a favorite restaurant, or the smell of a familiar meal, a previously learned response or experience can instantly be triggered.

Especially, if the previous experience was a favorable one.

I can't help but to wonder what Pavlov (a seminary dropout) would have to say about some of our **weekly altar calls.**

Especially those pertaining to areas outside of salvation.

Special Altar Calls for **Prayer.**
Special Altar Calls for **Deliverance.**
Special Altar Calls for **Forgiveness.**
Special Altar Calls for **Empowerment.**
Special Altar Calls for **Appointment.**

While I see nothing wrong with the above, when offered every week, I wonder how long it will take for these special altar calls to no longer be…

…well, **special.**

Although difficult to admit, many of us (as ministry leaders) actually enjoy being a **stimulus provider** for God.

For some reason, we have been conditioned to think that our worship services must always end the same way.

With an altar call.

Sadly, we have conditioned a brand new generation of believers who salivate whenever an altar call is made.

Regardless of whether they are (spiritually) hungry or not.

They have a phrase for that in Russia you know?
They call it **acondicionamiento clásico.**

Translation:
Classic conditioning.

Mr. Pavlov Himself

Heel Fear

It's truly amazing that while **76%** of our church congregations are nearly comprised of all women, very few actually hold **significant leadership** positions within the church.

As Mars Blackman would say:
"It's gotta be the shoes!"

Honorariums

I personally have no problem with churches who provide guest speakers or artists with some form of payment for the services they render.

That is more than honorable.
Hence the word.

However, just not sure if many of our churches know what the word '**honorarium**' actually means.

Honorarium derives from the Latin word, *honorarius,* which means a payment for a service (like public speaking) on which custom or propriety **forbids a price** to be set.

Simply put, honorariums were a *bestowed honor,* not the payment of a *prescribed fee.*

Big difference.

Honor due **upon request** is not honor at all.
Honor due and given **without request** is honor indeed.

If an artist or speaker requests a church to pay them a specific amount of money to render a particular service, then that exchange should not be called an honorarium.

That's called a bill.

Now seen on more packaging than USDA.

The Church Bookstore

On March 12, 2008, the Wall Street Journal published an interesting article on Borders Bookstores.

While most bookstores, in order to insure they can provide a greater inventory of books to their customers, adopt a **SPINE FACING OUT** book display sale strategy...

...Borders decided to do something different.

The popular bookstore chain made a decision to test a **FRONT FACING** book display selling strategy.

Spine Facing

Front Facing

In doing so, the management team of these stores discovered that several of their older books, primarily those that were no longer selling as much, had to be removed from the shelves in order to make room for newer or best-selling releases.

Well, can you guess what happened?

The following month's sales increased to over 9%!

In fact, their sales were so impressive that the bookstore chain decided to switch all of its stores to a front facing strategy.

Their breakthrough discovery:
Selected inventory vs. **Large inventory.**

So what does this have to do with your church's bookstore?

Well, several things.

1. Since most church bookstores are only open during worship service hours, a smart inventory strategy is paramount.

Why stock a book or a message series from five years ago if you're only open on Sunday(s)?

Maximize on what's current and fresh in the minds of your customers.

If you want to sell history, **sell it online.**

---

2. If you agree with the strategy listed above, then ask yourself:

Does our church even need a physical store on site to sell these products?

If we only focus on selling our current (or the previous month's) message series, is the creation and placement of **sale kiosks** a better option than a physical bookstore at our church?

Wow. My ears are starting to ring pretty loud now. Someone reading this is not at all happy with me.

I can just imagine how many church bookstore employees reading this are screaming for me to stop.

Trust me, I'm on your side.
(See The Traveling Salesman, page #122)

By decreasing your inventory, as well as adopting a better sale strategy, you can open a door for your church to do even **greater things** than struggling to staff a bookstore.

Especially when it's open only one day a week.

Church Payphones

Two things could be at work here.

Either we figured out we can raise some spare change from the one or two people left on earth…

…who do not have a cell phone.

Or either we've come to the sad conclusion that our church members may be too stingy to allow the one or two people left on earth, who do not have a cell phone…

…to use theirs.

Not a good look either way.

Trial Sermon

Not sure why we continue to use this cookie-cutter approach whenever someone makes a commitment to the ministry.

A **call to serve** does not always mean a **call to preach.**

I wonder how many potentially great leaders we have ruined because of this ancient rite of passage.

Pre-mature microphone exposure is a dangerous thing.

The Offering Plate

I am a big fan of the bucket.
Really wish more churches were too.

Using plates tends to make newcomers feel a bit awkward.

I've discovered that it is much easier for them to perform the
infamous '**empty hand**' offering drop technique with buckets.

Plates have a way of putting a newcomer's
financial business on blast for the whole pew to see.

I won't even mention how plates have a way of tempting a
newly appointed aisle usher to give their pew the evil eye.

*For those who still desire to use plates, be sure yours are
padded with that old school red velvet lining.*

Helps keep those coins from gossiping.

Sometimes I think we assume that every person who enters our doors is **a member.**

Only members, who have already bought into a vision of an organization, will tolerate the kind of bulletins we provide.

At least they will for a little while.

I looked up the word 'bulletin' in the dictionary the other day, and found these words:

A brief public notice issued usually from an authoritative source; a brief news item intended for immediate publication.

Boring.

Our ministry materials must always be created with the mindset that every person who enters our doors is **a visitor.**

Visitors don't need to be informed.
They need to be **impressed.**
In fact, they need to be blown away.

Here's an experiment you can try:

Take one of your previous church bulletins and bring it with you to a nearby Borders bookstore.

When you arrive, go immediately to the Arts & Photography section. Pull out a book entitled, **1000 Greetings** (by Peter King & Company).

After flipping through a few pages, take a look back at the bulletin you brought with you.

See where I'm going with this?

THE CHURCH BULLETIN

THE BRANDED PULPIT PODIUM

You can ask anyone who knows me.
My memory is terrible.

However, I can't recall a time when I've visited a church on Sunday, and after entering the sanctuary, immediately forgot the name of the church I was in.

Unless you know of a few people who do, placing the name of your church on the **pulpit podium** doesn't make a lot of sense.

That would be similar to my wife and I placing a sign on the door of our master bathroom that said:

Our Bathroom.

Not necessary.

Location Fever

Ever tried playing the board game **Memory**
without having all of the pieces inside the box?

No matter how hard you try, I promise you,
it is nearly an impossible task.

Yet year after year, churches all over the country are
planting **new locations** throughout their cities and
neighboring states that are now suffering due
to one (if not all) of the following:

Unpaired resources.
Unpaired facilities.

And worst of all, **unpaired leaders.**

Never underestimate the importance of assessing and
correcting systems, before trying to **duplicate them.**

Leveraging today's social media outlets and embracing
an **online video campus strategy** can not only enable more
churches to receive and aggregate the data necessary to
know where God may be leading them to possibly plant…

…but doing so just may help lower the number of speeding
tickets some of our pastors keep getting from trying to drive
from location to location every Sunday to speak to us.

Quick Tip: *Stream there* before *going there.*

As a child, I found grammar to be difficult at times.

Nouns. Adjectives. Verbs. At times, they all looked alike to me.

Step inside some of our churches, and you'll see I'm not alone.

I understand how we can **BE** the church. I understand how we can **ATTEND** a church.

But how exactly does someone **HAVE** church?

That phrase troubles me every time I hear it.

THE LET'S HAVE
CHURCH
PHRASE

Numerology

I am a strong believer in the significance of **numbers** when it comes to many of the divine plans of God.

However, using them every Sunday in our messages may not be the best thing for our recovering gambling converts.

Some may try to find the rationale in buying a ticket with the number of **completion** and **perfection**, along with a bit of **grace** and **agreement**, all of course, in the year of **new beginnings.**

Translation: **3 7 5 2 8**

(By the way, please don't try that one. I did already.)

71

Telling Your Neighbor Something

But asking our members every five minutes to turn and *"tell their neighbor something"* can be a bit annoying.

Especially when they're the only one on their pew.

Midweek Worship Services

While I used to be one a while back,
I unfortunately am no longer a big fan of them.

Not because I dislike the purpose.
Just think the learning method is a little off.

Consider this:

According to a recent study performed by
The National Training Laboratories (Bethel, Maine),
the following are some average **learning retention rates**
for today's average student...

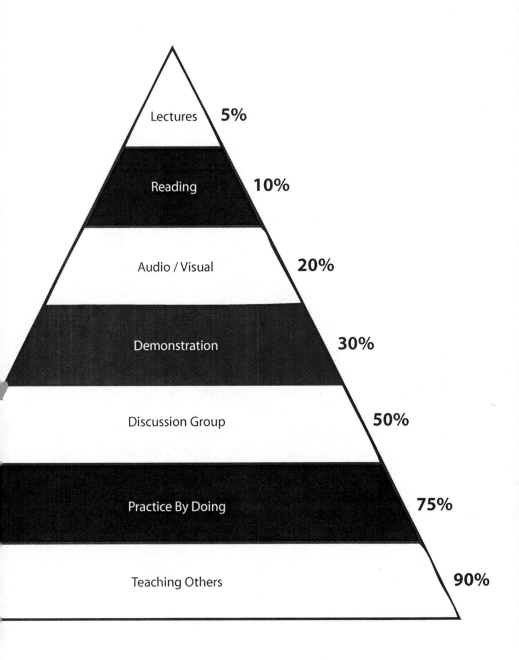

Lectures 5%

Reading 10%

Audio / Visual 20%

Demonstration 30%

Discussion Group 50%

Practice By Doing 75%

Teaching Others 90%

Isn't it interesting that the highest retention rates involve some form of **small group study** or discipleship application?

As you can see, midweek worship services may keep the lights on, but not always **the ears.** Try small groups instead.

The Athletic Ministry

As an intense sports lover, this one may
seem a bit odd coming from me.

So allow me to first submit this small disclaimer:

If your church has a **GO THERE & PLAY**
athletic ministry model, then I absolutely would embrace it.

But if your church has a **COME HERE & PLAY**
athletic ministry model, then it's probably time to get rid of it.

As a father of three, nothing would please me more than
for my children to grow up knowing that not everyone
they meet (and compete with) **prays** before they play.

Here's a small recommendation:

Join leagues.
Don't create them.

Sports are great tools for us
to burst bubbles with.

Not remain in them.

The Laymember Conference

Which do you prefer?
The **machine gun** or the **rifle?**

Try to relax: this is not a hidden invitation
from me to join the NRA.

Just curious as to which ministry approach you believe
is more suitable when it comes to **conferences.**

You see, there used to be a time when church
conferences were primarily *for leaders.*

But now more often that not, churches are creating conferences
that are geared for *those they lead.*

While the former is focused on **equipping.**
The latter is often focused on **inspiring.**

The danger with laymember conferences is that sooner or later, churches fall into the temptation of inviting speakers because of their ability *to draw*, versus their ability *to equip*.

I've seen my share of both, and no matter where I go, it seems the intended focus and expected results tend to be the same.

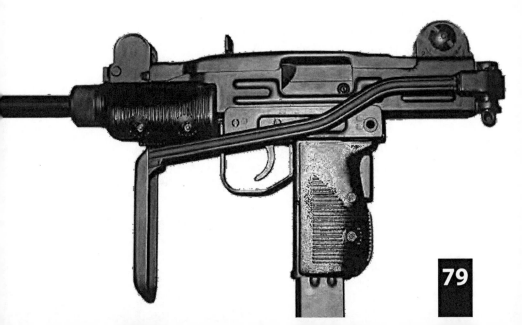

Laymember conferences:
Machine Gun Approach

Non-Laymember conferences:
Rifle Approach

While one needs **a crowd** in order to be considered effective, the other is in need of a **specific target.**

While one thrives **on noise** and the emptying of shells, the other thrives on **precision** and **focus.**

(Again I ask) Which do you prefer?

POLITICIAN DAY

Said I'll be gone 'til November, I'll be gone 'til November
Yo, tell my girl, I'll be gone til November
January, February, March, April, May
I see you cryin, but girl, I can't stay
I'll be gone til November, I'll be gone til November
Yo, tell my girl, I'll be gone til November

Wouldn't it be just the coolest thing to have **Wyclef Jean**
as a member of your church? Especially during election season?

Commit to providing Sunday morning recognition,
only after aspiring politicians agree to host special
Saturday morning community forums. At your church.

Our vote must be worth more than **an annual wave offering.**

Vacation Bible School

What wise guy thought these three words
could actually go together?

The whole thing seems like an oxymoron.
Especially to kids.

No matter the age, **kids love vacation.**
As for school, *not so much.*

Maybe it's time we get a bit more creative when it comes
to the **ministry programs** we provide over the summer.

The Church Building Fund

Every church at some point in its lifespan will
undergo some form of capital campaign or building fund.

It's inevitable.
Growth *(no matter how you look at it)* will have **a cost.**

There is however one building fund method that
I believe we may need to re-examine its effectiveness.

While it has been passed down now for several generations,
I am convinced it does not need to be passed around any longer.

This new **P Generation** just does not have the stomach for it.

(P Generation? Turn to page 112 for more about them)

The building fund method I'm referring to is:
The Carrot, Horse, & Cart Strategy

I'm sure you're pretty familiar with it:

Church, Here's Our Need **(carrot)**
Church, Here's The Cost **(cart)**
Church, Will You Help Us? **(horse)**

By and large, this strategy has
worked for many in the past.

But for many churches today,
it is no longer working.

While I don't want to assume to be an expert in these matters (because I most certainly am not), I believe for many, this strategy has ceased from working simply because it is **NEED-BASED.**

Today's generation are no longer attracted to needs. And no, it's not because they're selfish.

This generation **LOVES** to give.

But their giving today is rarely based on needs. Their giving is based on **vision.**

A **STRATEGICALLY** planned-out vision.

If your church has to have a specific church building fund of some sort every year, or every other year for that matter…

…there may not be a money problem at all.

There may be a vision problem.

The Overflow Area

Mark my words.

In just a few more years, we are going to have to convince some late Sunday arrivals that the **'overflow area'** is not in any way related to something *spiritual*.

Please.

Just call that area your **'rear'** or **'additional'** seating space.

Much simpler to explain.

The Church MySpace Page

I am a big fan of technology.
Huge fan actually.

Especially when it comes to new online media outlets
like blogs and social networking sites.

However, only when they are used **the right way.**

With the emergence of such social networking websites
like Facebook, YouTube, and Twitter, not to mention the
112 million people worldwide who now have their own blogs,
it is clear that the times of modern communication have changed.

Yet despite the number of businesses and civic organizations
who have embraced this new era of interactive media and
marketing methods to reach their respective audiences,
there remains one that seems to be lagging way behind:

The Local Church.

While more and more churches continue to place their faith (and budgets) in old media outlets like magazine ads, billboards, direct mail and radio and TV campaigns, it is this new era of online media that is now impacting the lives of today's generation.

However, one of the biggest mistakes any church can make is to try to engage with this new media era without fully understanding it.

Doing so can be foolish.

Since most churches are still fairly new to this game, I decided to interview someone who is not.

During the spring of 2008, I had the opportunity to interview best-selling author and marketing consultant **Seth Godin** about a book he wrote entitled, *Meatball Sundae.*

*Required reading for any ministry leader who desires to leverage new media today on behalf of the local church.

In Meatball Sundae, Seth unveils how businesses and organizations, who have been quite successful in the past, are now faced with trying to change their existing structures to embrace new social marketing tactics and methods.

So, before you rush to create that church Facebook or MySpace page, please read this...

Me: Your new book is entitled Meatball Sundae. I'm scared to ask…what is a meatball sundae? Sounds disgusting.

Seth (Godin): It is disgusting. It's disgusting because it's the combination of two perfectly good things.

Meatballs--standard items, things we've always used, things made in quantity and aimed at the masses, together with the Sundae--the social media, Facebook, blogs and all that new online marketing stuff that people are so excited about.

Meatballs are just fine. An ordinary church service for the neighborhood is fine. But it won't lead to growth. And if you add something just fine to the revolutionary new media tools we've got, it just doesn't work.

The book is a message to marketers everywhere (including churches, who are marketers too) that if you want to play in this new world, you need to understand the new rules and you need to make a new product.

Me: It seems like everyone is into this "new marketing" era or as you like to call it, "sundae toppings." Why do you think that is?

Seth: Well, when it works, it works amazingly well.

Presidential candidates get millions of viewers, every day on YouTube, for free. Sites like Twitter.com double in size every few months. It feels like old marketing but for free, and better and faster.

So it's seductive. But it doesn't work for most organizations. It especially doesn't work for boring ones.

Me: Your definition of the "old marketing" era sounds a lot like what many businesses and churches are still stuck doing today.

Why do you think the "new marketing" is not embraced as much?

Seth: Churches are the oldest businesses around today. And yes, they are businesses.

They don't necessarily sell a physical product, and they don't always charge money, but there's a transaction nonetheless.

And that involves the individual paying attention. Attention is precious and it's rare and it's non-refundable.

Old organizations relish tradition and often fight change. But new media (and the growth it brings with it) requires change, because no one is going to choose to talk about you merely because you are old and safe and proven. It's not worth talkin about, not as much as something fashionable, new or interesting.

Me: Seth, There are a few churches out there who have begun to embrace this "new marketing" era; flirting around with MySpace, Facebook, and some have even begun posting worship service videos on YouTube.

However, many still feel like the new marketing isn't working for them. Is there a step somewhere they seem to be missing?

Seth: Why would I spend the time to watch something on YouTube if I knew what was going to happen?

Why would I friend someone on FaceBook if I knew that all they intended to do was hassle me and evangelize to me?

Just because it's important to you (and it could be your Tupperware product line or your sermon) doesn't mean it's important to me. The essential idea here is that new media is selfish and you can't buy or demand attention, no matter how worthy you believe your idea may be.

Me: One big area many churches have yet to embrace is blogging. Foreign and often viewed as tedious to many church leaders, you view it as a major tool to winning and consistently serving a particular audience.

Can you explain further?

Seth: Blogging lets you drip ideas, bit by bit, to people who want to hear them. There are two crucial ideas in that sentence, so let's unpack them.

The dripping matters because that's how people learn. Not in one hour chunks, but one little idea at a time.

Do it for five years or more, every single day (as I've done on my blog) and you build trust and credibility and a body of work.

The permission ("want to hear them") is important because if no one is reading your blog, you'll know. And then you can change it. And over time, you can earn the right to talk to a thousand and then ten thousand and then a million people.

And isn't that your mission?

Me: Yep Seth. It sure is.

Before trying to jump into land of space or face, I highly recommend creating a blog or a **Twitter account.**

Especially one for your pastor or staff.

Update it regularly and you may be surprised at how your congregation over time will love to follow along with you.

While Facebook is a superb connection tool, it can quickly give you a **false sense** of community building.

The speed of connection and community are very different.

Either way, consider creating a **Facebook Fan Page** for your church. And please, whatever you do, leave MySpace alone.

Mr. Murdoch did a great job of sinking that platform and media strategy.

And if you're not careful, **you'll sink right along with it.**

Multi-Ethnic Stock Photography

Do you know any of these people?

If you don't, it's okay.
I don't either. In fact, most churches don't.

But day after day, most churches insist they do.
They plaster them on their websites, their bulletins,
their banners, and just about every flyer or mailer you
receive from them. *Still don't know any these people?*

Well, allow me to introduce you to the good folks
from the land of **stock photography!**

These fine folk can be found (and purchased) at any online
photo store, ready and willing to join your church temporarily
to advertise its events and programs! *Is that convenient or what?*

With photo purchase prices ranging from $1 to $349, you too
can make church ads look happy, exciting, and heck,
maybe even **multicultural.**

*Trust me on this one: Stock photography cannot and
will not out wrestle old traditions.*

For those who use stock photography,
please beware of the following two challenges:

The first: Your members have never seen or met these
people before. They've tried, but can't seem to find them.

The second: That guy in the Viagra ad I saw in the paper
the other day looks just like that guy you used on your men's
prayer breakfast flyer. *What a strange coincidence, right?*

Be different. **Use your people.**

95

Conference Offerings

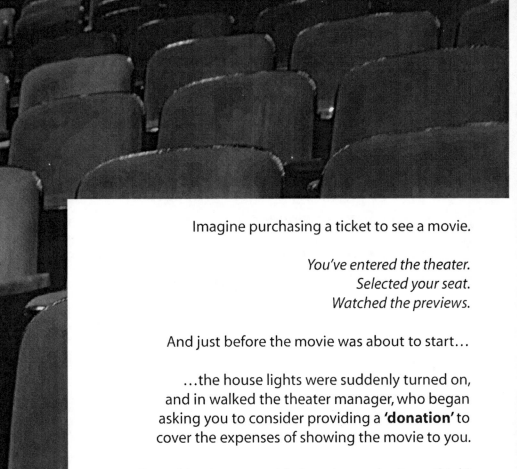

Imagine purchasing a ticket to see a movie.

You've entered the theater.
Selected your seat.
Watched the previews.

And just before the movie was about to start…

…the house lights were suddenly turned on, and in walked the theater manager, who began asking you to consider providing a **'donation'** to cover the expenses of showing the movie to you.

Something is wrong with that picture, don't you think?

If your church conference has a registration cost to attend, then raising an **'offering'** should not be necessary.

Offerings during a conference should always be to *advance* a particular cause, not to *correct* one.

When preparing your conference budget, two things a church should always remember to do:

Book less and **charge right.**

Mission ~~Statement~~
Paragraphs

If your church mission statement is made up of more
than 12 words, it may be time to come up with a new one.

Paragraphs don't inspire.
They confuse.

And consequently, they are quickly forgotten.

Don't believe me?
Ask your staff.

Church Business Directory

If church members desire to support one another in business, that's perfectly fine.

Just let them find each other on their own.

I've seen a few altar calls in my day turn into steel cage matches when a painter's invoice remained unpaid or when the wheel alignment on a deacon's pickup truck still wasn't fixed right.

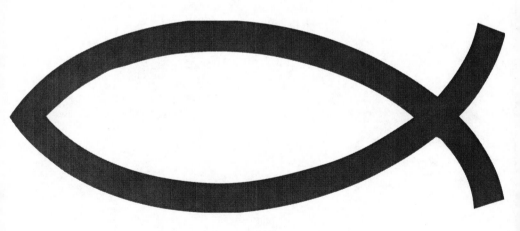

I realize supporting your own may have value, but **Ichthys stamped** business cards don't mean as much these days.

DOV

Want a sure-fire way to keep (today's) men away
from our churches, particularly our church websites?

Shower it with doves.

Yesterday's symbol of faith is today's symbol of skin care.

For the sake of all manhood:
Try something else.

100

The Church Choir

I know you probably didn't expect to see this one here.
I'm sure it will take a whole book to convince you of this one.

Didn't have time to write one just yet, but here are **TEN** reasons
why I think we may need to get rid of the choir.

10. Hollywood and the business community will have to think a bit more critically when trying to reach the urban Christian market regarding their products.

9. Sunday offering will go up by about 67 people. *Apparently, robe pockets are too small these days for wallets.*

8. We already have a praise and worship team. Let them sing.

7. The congregation will now sound a lot better.

6. Empty space will allow room for great visual presentations. *Turn the page to see what I mean.*

imagine the possibilities.

the guys over at //**renewedvision.com** are a beast.

5. Falling asleep in the pews (rather than choir stand) won't be as much of a distraction.

4. The whole sectional singing spotlight thing is so 80's. *"...Sopranos...now the altos..*

3. The director's robe is getting **more raves** than the pastor's.

2. The other 57 ministries in the church can now have more than **three active members.**

and finally...

1. Sunday morning worship can now be cut down to an hour;

a goal I encourage your church to strive for if you desire
to reach the unchurched in your surrounding community.

Symphonies, while magnificent to the ear, are rarely attended
more than once by the average music lover.

While some find the beauty of music simply irresistible,
others prefer the beauty of **time management.**

Find the balance in those two and your church
will have something great on its hands.

Try losing the choir for 3 months.
Let's just see what happens.

107

Praying For The Sick & Shut-In

Shocked by this one? If so, allow me to explain.

There indeed is a great importance for our churches
to lift the names of those who are **sick or shut-in** in prayer.

Nothing can delight God more.

But before we copy and paste the same group of names
to the bulletin we've been praying for over the last six Sundays,
we may need to take a look down the pew every once and a while.

Sister Jenkins has been back for a few months now.

On a more serious note:
Leaders, pay attention to prayer requests.

If every time you gather for prayer, your requests seem to
only be for those who are sick, you may need to call a time-out.

Announcement: The church is not a hospital.

The more you allow it to become one,
the more it will need to be sanitized.

When was the last time someone asked you for prayer regarding
someone who was lost? Or for the vision of your church?

Our prayer requests need to mature. **Now.**

Flash

I am sure you and I would both agree that 'flashing' someone is extremely inappropriate and illegal.

Yet, surprising enough, I know a few churches who commit to doing it all the time.

No. I'm not talking about 'flashing' in terms of sexual misbehavior.

But rather the 'flashing' that some of our church website designers are trying to add way too much of these days.

Yes. **Adobe Flash** is an awesome tool.
(I remember when it was just good ole' Macromedia!)

And yes, seeing your church, pastor, or maybe even Jesus Himself flying across the screen can get a few people excited.
(Well, maybe not the flying Jesus part!)

But you know what's cooler than that?

Content.

Regularly updated (and user-friendly) content.

You'd be surprised how many churches will spend top dollar to create flashy website intros that people just love to skip.

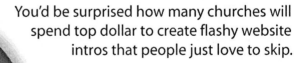

Super Bowl Parties

Remember:
The game is only once a year.

Please, consider giving your youth leaders **a break.**

Or better yet, discover what churches or recreational centers in your neighborhood are also hosting a Super Bowl party.

And partner with them.

Besides, the commercials are not nearly as funny via TiVo.

If you just have to throw one, let's make it a priority to call a nearby sports bar and arrange a party for **the parents** too.

May cost a few bucks, but at least you won't have to wait all night for that last parent to finally decide to pick up their child.

And all the youth leaders said…**Amen!**

GENERATION P

The following article appeared in the
New York Times on May 9, 2008.

Just in case your church is still labeling
this generation as **Generation X**, or **Y,**
please read this!

" Whether it's Sarah Silverman singing about a media buyer or Stephen Colbert breathing deeply from a bag of Doritos, MTV Networks sure knows how to impress advertisers.

At its upfront presentation in New York on Thursday, the owners of MTV, VH1, Comedy Central, Nickelodeon, CMT and other cable channels pushed a multi-screen strategy.

Judy McGrath, the chairman of MTV Networks, introduced yet another moniker for the youth generation, **"Generation P,"** describing them as **"the young adults who expect to produce and program their own media."**

"We're moving with them freely across every screen," she said. "Our fans aren't merely consuming his stuff, they're more invested and engaged than ever."

At the start of the presentation, Jon Stewart, host of "The Daily Show" on Comedy Central, talked about advertising with his usual deadpan delivery.

"I thought we didn't do these anymore!," Mr. Stewart joked. "I thought that was the point of the writers' strike."

Later, he laughed about the "impressionable" 18 to 34 year-old viewers that MTV Networks attracts, saying:

"They trust us. And I think you can exploit that."

article above written by Brian Stelter

113

The Singing Preacher

We give praise to God for the gift.

We would also give praise to God if the gift did not **always** have to conclude a message.

It never fails.

The more the *call to preach* is merged with the *gift to sing,* the more **the latter** is often celebrated.

Don't believe me?

Ask a singing preacher
to release an album.

And a message series.

At the same time.

Receipts never lie.

The Quest For Maturity

About a year or so ago, I was meeting with a friend
for lunch who happened to be a worship leader
for a local church located in Atlanta, Georgia.

Before we could even give our order to our waitress,
he began to share the struggle he was having with leading
his church into what he called a **'corporate'** worship.

He discussed how it seemed that there was always a group
of people that he had to *instruct* to stand, *beg* for them to lift
their hands, and despite how he tried to select songs that he
thought everyone in the church would know…

…there would be people that (in his mind) would refuse
to sing and *participate* along with him.

And then he uttered these five words, words that have become
a **QUEST** that churches all over the globe today
(in my opinion) are consumed with:

"We must become more MATURE."

After telling our waitress to come back once again
(since we had yet to look at the menu), I told him it may be
time to reconsider what he and other leaders just like him
believe a **MATURE** church really looks like.

I explained to him that the word 'mature' is actually defined
as being **fully developed**, and ripe for reproduction.

Anything that has become mature, when reproduction occurs,
the end result is not increased maturity. But in fact, **immaturity.**

Had my incredibly beautiful wife Imani ever delivered our three children as three mature, fully aged adults, the judges for the Guinness Book of World Records would have surely named us both the **'Freaks of the Millennium.'**

I can see the headline on The New York Post reading something like this: *"Mother Delivers Three Full Grown Adults, Not Babies."*

Just the thought of something like that happening makes my stomach hurt. Not to mention the stomach of my wife.

Anyone seeking for a mature church, must understand and embrace that the first sign of true maturity, is the **abundance of immaturity.**

I realize that this may sound strange, but if everyone in your church is in the choir, on the usher board, a faithful tither, has never missed a service, and is just in love with the pastor…

…your church may just be on the brink of death.

Our churches should always be full of *'babes'* in Christ, who seem to always be whining and complaining about the challenges of life, because that's just what babies do.

As a father of three, I am doing the best I can not to spank my children for something I have never fully taught them.

As the one who is considered the most **MATURE** in the house, my job is to learn how to cultivate an environment of growth.

If everyone in your church **GETS IT,** then you might as well close the doors, because it is apparent that no one is now committed to going out and bringing in those who don't.

Needless to say, we had a pretty quiet lunch after that.

The Tambourine

Other than being one of the most annoying musical instruments God ever inspired man to create, **the tambourine** is often always used by that one ex-choir member that insists he or she was good enough to be playing in the band.

Not to mention that it is nearly impossible to keep a tambourine quiet during the message.

Somehow, someway…

…*it always seems to have at least one more jingle left.*

Christmas
Worship Service

Do I believe the meaning of Christmas has been lost and traded in by many church goers for gifts and presents? **Sure.**

But hosting a service on Christmas Day isn't going to help.

Give your staff and volunteers the greatest present you possibly can give them: **a break.**

If the budget needs a little help, pick at least two Sundays in the year to set aside funds for the holiday season drop-off.

Relax. Take time to enjoy your family.
The one you have at home.

Pew Dedications

I'm a strong believer in giving honor where honor is due.
I see nothing wrong with that at all.

However, when the efforts bleed into **dedicating** chairs
or rows of pews to the faithful, things can get a bit weird.

I remember standing near the back of one particular church and
I promise you, the sanctuary looked like the inside of a **mausoleum.**

Every chair had on its back the name of a member who had either
gone on to be with the Lord, or of one who had given a
considerable contribution to the church.

If we have to dedicate something at the church, let's try doing
so with something that won't cause as much of a **distraction.**

The whole dedicated chair or pew thing
has been known to start a riot or two.

Especially for those who are still living, who refuse to move
down the aisle because they insist on sitting in *"their seat."*

Voicemail

Confession: I hate the telephone.

I realize hate is a rather strong word, but for some reason or another, whether I am at home or at work, I rarely pick it up.

The same is true with my cell phone.

While it stays with me most of the day, the ringer is never on. **Never.**

Now on the other hand, send me an email or a text message, and I'll respond to it immediately. Pretty sad, right?

I've been asked by friends and colleagues alike about this and I've only seemed to come up with two theories:

1. Either this internet / instant message / social networking age is making me increasingly more *impersonal*.

or **2.** I've become allergic to the *gift of gab*.

I realize I'm not alone. Ministry leaders, as well as the churches they attend, have stopped answering the telephone.

And worst. They've stopped returning **voice messages.**

If you're still waiting for a call you left with the church's secretary last month to be returned, please, don't be angry.

It's not personal.
It's a growing epidemic.
And we need help.

The Traveling Salesman

If your church has already paid for a speaker or artist to render a service to your congregation, than you've done your duty.

But providing **FREE** access at your venue for the same speaker or artist (that you've already paid) to sell products to your church membership for **PROFIT,** is probably going beyond the call of duty.

To all my church bookstore owners:
I feel you're pain.

Exposure deserves some form of percentage.

The Homeless Ministry

I realize the following is a rather bold request.
But it's still worth a try.

If the **HOMELESS** you are serving are still **HOMELESS** after encountering your **HOMELESS** ministry month after month…

…then maybe it's time we try doing something else.

Contrary to popular opinion, the church is not in the business of providing fish. Or frying fish for that matter.

But rather to teach (and train) others how to catch fish.

What are some of the first things you would deem absolutely necessary if I asked you to teach someone how to fish?

Boats? *Yes.*
Fishing Rods? *Yes.*
Nets? *Sure.*
Bait? *Absolutely.*

Notice what is not listed above? **Fish.**

Our churches must become (and be known) as agents of **RADICAL** change, rather than just **TEMPORAL** ones.

Believe it or not, radical change can actually cost less than temporal change, if one chooses to invest in it early enough.

You only need to purchase a boat or rod once if your goal is to teach and train. However, you will have to purchase fish every day if your goal is only to feed temporarily.

Quick Observation:
There is never enough money for *temporal* change.

I am sure we all can name several civic agencies and organizations in our communities that are great at providing some **TEMPORAL** change to those who are homeless.

Instead of becoming them.
Support them.

Our goals are very different.
And our funding must be as well.

The
Double
Title Method

Ever had to introduce someone as *The Rev. Dr.?*
Presiding Bishop?
Or perhaps the *General Overseer?*

Or my personal favorite: **The Right Reverend?**

Maybe we should just use *one title* at a time.

Newcomers have a hard enough time with
some of our church names.

Sidenote: If you already have at least one denomination
within your church name, please do not add another.

Way too confusing.

Powerpoint

Ask anyone who knows me.

They'll be quick to tell you that I am a big believer and admirer of visual ministry presentations.

However, as a Mac user for several years now, nothing can make the hair on my back stand straight up than to see a church use **Microsoft Powerpoint** to assist during worship.

And I don't even have any hair there.

When it comes to worship enhancement, please be sure to introduce your techees to *Keynote* or *ProPresenter*.

(check out page #104 to see ProPresenter in action)

I guarantee they'll place a little more **power** behind your point.

127

Annual Themes

Allow me to clarify this. I think it's perfectly fine for
our churches to have a yearly **theme** for itself or its members.

But please. Don't place an ad *publicizing* your theme.

Flip through any Christian magazine or church television
network and the ads you'll find there will make you
think our God has become **schizophrenic.**

With every church and pastor declaring a different theme
for God's people to follow, one can't help but wonder
who God is actually talking to.

Or through.

Devil Love

I remember driving in traffic one day and turning to a popular gospel radio station here in Atlanta.

They were playing *"Friend of God"* by Israel Houghton. Great song. Awesome artist. **One truly incredible message.**

Although I don't do gospel radio stations much, I decided to go ahead and finish listening to the song.

Then came a different song. From a different artist.

The artist must have named *"the devil"* at least **32 times** before I decided to shut it off. No joke (I counted).

The essence of the song was to *"take back"* everything he has *"stolen"* from us as believers.

Don't really want to get into too much theological discussion here, but I have to say that there has to come a time when the songs we sing, especially within our churches, are **fixated** on the name and nature of God.

And not his foe.

Just think that it's about time we move beyond him.

I think **Dick Gregory** said it best. As a panelist for Tavis Smiley's State Of The Black Union back in 2008, he said…

"…my momma was so busy telling me about the devil, I was a grown man before I found out about the beauty of God."

Let's show the world how much we've grown. Please. Ease up on all the **devil love.**

watch

On the evening of **December 31, 1862,** churches and homes
all over the nation were filled with slaves praying and earnestly
awaiting the news that President Abraham Lincoln
would finally deliver on his promise.

Well, on the stroke of **midnight**, January 1st, 1863, he did.

The Emancipation Proclamation became a law, declaring
that all slaves in the Confederate states were now 'legally' free.

After nearly 145 years, this tradition of gathering on the last
night of the year together in houses of worship has been kept
by many African-Americans as a way of not only celebrating the
dawning of a new year, but also as a way of demonstrating a sense
of gratitude to God for the year that has passed.

Question: So what's wrong with that?
Answer: Absolutely nothing.

I am one who wholeheartedly believes in the importance of
keeping this cultural and faith-driven tradition alive.

It is undeniable that the era of slavery here in America did a great
job of stripping away so much; so I am pleased this one tradition
found a way to slip through the cracks.

I just wish we could call it by another name.

I realize I may only be 33, and still have much I need to learn, but if there is one thing I know to be true in life, it is this:

Position can at times trump Purpose.
(I think I may say that again later in this book; see page #148)

It is extremely difficult to stretch towards the future, when you are still positioned according to your past.

Long before the evening of December 31, 1862, it was custom for African slaves to gather together on the last night of the year because January 1st was also the day that many slave owners began to tally up their accounts for the year.

Land, furnishings, and yes, human property were often sold in order to satisfy debts on that day, causing many slaves to be separated from their family, never to see each other again.

So historically, there is an understood position and posture of expectancy among African-Americans that on New Year's Eve, we look to God, and flock to many of our churches, in order to hear a message of hope and assurance that the year to come will prayerfully be a favorable one.

night

My wife will probably attest to the fact that on any given day of the week, if asked, I will claim a different passage of scripture as my all-time favorite.

At the time I wrote this book, this one was at the top of the list:

> *But before faith came, we were kept **under guard** by the law, kept for the faith which would afterward be revealed.*
>
> *Therefore the law was our tutor to bring us to Christ, that we might be justified by faith.*
>
> *But after faith has come, we are **no longer** under a tutor.*
>
> **- Galatians 3:23-25**

By continuing to call this annual tradition **"Watch Night,"** I can't help but to wonder if we are fostering a system of faith that is still bound and under the guard of an old law; a law and belief system that renews in many of us an unhealthy pattern of **spiritual slavery,** one that causes many to wait all year long for someone (in the flesh) to make a declaration that we are free.

news flash:

In Christ, we have **ALREADY** been made free.

As believers, we are no longer under a tutor.

There is nothing as sons and daughters of God, joint-heirs with Christ Jesus, that we need to *'wait'* and *'watch'* for on the last night of the year, that God will not reveal to us in faith on any other day of the year.

So, is it okay to gather on New Year's Eve to celebrate?

Absolutely.

But maybe we should embrace a new name for that evening's celebration. I think I've got just the name too.

How about…**New Year's Eve?**
(you have to admit, it does have a catchy ring to it!!)

The Armor Bearer

A small glass of water can weigh somewhere in the neighborhood of **8 to 14 ounces.**

A brand new copy of The NKJV Bible
(before highlights and tabs)
can weigh anywhere between **1 to 2 pounds.**

And a non-tailored suit jacket (four buttons only), will rarely weigh more than **3 to 5 pounds.**

Here's one more interesting fact:

The primitive body armor worn and carried by soldiers dating as early as 3000 B.C., usually consisted of the following:

Coat Of Mail.   Habergeon.
Brigandine.   Breastplate.
Stomach Belt.   and A Girdle.

Although it may take me a few Google searches, I'd be very surprised if armor bearing back then was less than a **250+ pound** dragging job.

Weapons not included.

So, what am I saying? If it doesn't **weigh** the same thing, don't **call** it the same thing.

Try personal assistant instead.

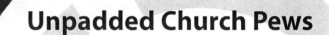

Unpadded Church Pews

Is there anything more cruel?

Making people sit on one of these for one, two,
or sometimes three-hour services can be **pure torture.**

Waterboarding is child's play compared to this.

Our fine folks at Gitmo can surely pick up
a *few good tricks* watching us.

Televised Worship Services

Not that I am a huge fan of **Reality TV**, but doesn't it seem like everyone is doing reality television *except* for the church?

Ever wonder if there is anything else we can be showing other than **church worship services?**

Sometimes I wonder if we've forgotten *one simple truth:*

The people we want to **watch** our worship services are the same people who are **not attending** our worship services.

Believe it or not, television is an **old model.**

One that is extremely over priced,
and extremely difficult to measure results from.

Utilizing the internet to provide *live streaming*
or archived video of your messages is a much better
resource to keep people connected throughout the week.

Your church's immediate ROI can be **tracked online.**
But it can't through TV.

If you insist on showing your services on TV, take the time to
sit down and watch your televised services along with your
church leadership in an effort to answer this one question:

"Is this really the first thing we want the
unchurched to see: **a worship service?**"

We've got to be more creative than this.

Sidenote: Broadcast just your messages,
not the entire worship service.

Worship environments are difficult to replicate
over the web. Especially two to three hours worth.

Hammond B3

Based upon my light research, the **Hammond B3** organ turns 75 years old this year.

75 years old!

While I'm not a betting man, I'm sure odds are its founder, Laurens Hammond, never thought we would have kept his organ around this long.

Well Laurens, take a bow.

Even though the last (electromechanical) version came off the assembly line in the mid '70s, many of us now believe it is impossible to **hear** or **feel God** without it on Sunday.

Congratulations.

Youth Sunday

Or as I used to call it when I was a child: **"yuf sunday."**

This is that often celebrated time of the year when churches all across the country permit their children or students to facilitate certain facets of the Sunday adult worship service.

As a young child growing up in the church, I have to admit, I was always a **huge fan** of Youth Sunday.

Just thought it was the coolest thing in the world for me and my friends to get a chance to run things for a whole Sunday just like the grown ups would do.

It wasn't until years later, during a trip to the local zoo with my family, that I realized how **unproductive** this ritual really was.

I'll never forget that day. Probably because my wife thought it would be a great idea to go to the Atlanta zoo on **Father's Day.**

Father's Day is in June.
June (in Atlanta) is hot.

Ungodly hot.

As we walked around the zoo that day, fanning ourselves
and spending a fortune on beverages for the girls,
we approached the popular **Giant Panda** exhibit.

Behind a glass wall (probably a few inches thick)
lay these two beautiful creatures,
each probably weighing at least 200 lbs.

I believe their names were **Mei Lan** and **Xi Lan.**

The exhibit was full of wall-to-wall people,
so much so, I had to hoist our oldest on
my shoulders just to get a peek.

What she saw *confused* her.
And later on that day, confused me as well.

Both of the pandas were busy chewing on several of
the bamboo sticks lying around them on the floor.

But they were doing so...
...with their BACKS turned to the glass.

No matter how much the people next to us were shouting
out their names or banging their hands on the glass,
the pandas would not turn around.

After we left the exhibit, my daughter, now a little
disappointed, asked why the pandas would
not turn around so she could see them.

I replied (just as most know-it-all fathers would) with...

... *"They were eating baby.
They probably just didn't want to be disturbed."*

For some reason, although she seemed to accept it,
that explanation just didn't sit right with me.

When we got home, I decided to look online and find out a little bit more about the pandas we saw there at the zoo.

Come to find out, both of the pandas we saw there that morning were actually **born inside** the zoo.

In fact, they were born about two years apart from one another (2006 & 2008), and they were two of only five births that have occurred in a United States zoo over the past six years.

I'm sure you're wondering why this is at all important or relevant to a Youth Sunday. So I'll get to the point.

I wonder what would happen if both of those pandas were born in their **natural environment?**

An environment that wasn't as sterile.
An environment that wasn't as controlled.
An environment that wasn't as tame.

I'm sure if they were, their reaction to a room full of humans yelling at them and disturbing them while they eat would have been a bit different. Pandas can actually be very aggressive.

And deadly, if approached in the wrong manner.

Today, I encounter more and more of my peers,
who have grown up as children in church,
who no longer are aggressive when it comes to
matters of faith and the local church.

They have become sterile.
They have become easy to control.
And it many instances, they are indeed tame.

What happened to this generation?

Could it be that (over the years) this generation has
been raised somehow to believe that their **CORPORATE**
involvement in the local church is only to sing in a choir?

Or to dance?
Maybe be a part of some step or drama team?

While these things are indeed great outlets at times,
they often rarely demonstrate the **unique giftedness**
and intelligence young people have to offer the local church.

And its leadership.

Instead of hosting a Youth Sunday,
where adults can find joy in watching their
children perform in a sterile environment…

…why not unleash them to encounter God
in their own natural environments?

How do you do that, you ask?

It's simple.
DOUBLE THE YOUTH MINISTRY BUDGET.

For many churches, you may need to **TRIPLE** it.

Dare to radically change the landscape of your church and its campus by carving out the space necessary for your youth and students to flourish and be themselves.

By themselves.

In fact, I'll give you this one small token of advice:

If your adult sanctuary and classrooms have a combined **larger square footage** than what you have allocated for your youth...

...your church and ministry is *already* in decline.

No special day, event, or trip can serve as a substitute for allocated space. Space that is not only allocated, *but dedicated.*

Remember this: Reaching adults does not always guarantee reaching their kids. However, reaching kids will **always** guarantee reaching their parents (the adults).

'Cause somebody's got to drive them!

Pastor Booking Pages

If found on the pastor's *personal* ministry website:

Cool.

If found on the pastor's *church* website
(particularly its home page):

Not cool.

Give people the benefit of the doubt.

If a church desires to invite a particular pastor to preach,
I'm pretty sure they'll do one of the following every time:

Write.
Call.
Email.
*(or for all of my fellow Twitter junkies: **DM**)*

Trust me: Placing a **booking page** on your church website
for your pastor can create a laundry list of problems.

Securing an outside agency (or enlisting a spouse) to
handle your pastor's speaking requests will insure that
your church executive office will always remain busy
keeping your pastor's head and hands **lifted up.**

And not out.

Church
Billboards

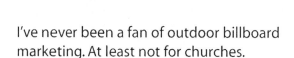

I've never been a fan of outdoor billboard marketing. At least not for churches.

While I can provide a pretty long list as to why I don't, I'll discuss **only two** for the sake of time and discussion.

1. The Moving Target.

Aside from those located near traffic stops, most outdoor billboards can only be seen when people are engaged in some form of *rapid movement*.

And of those seen, very few are read.

Outdoor billboards near transit areas are best used when attempting **to shock** an audience.

Not to inform one.

If your outdoor (transit area) billboard contains more than 15 words, consider yourself **an informer.**

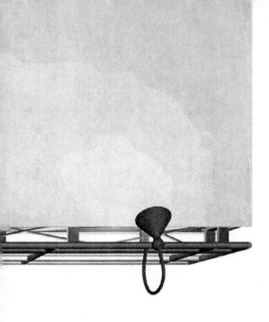

2. An Immovable Message.

Companies that sell outdoor billboard space often require *multi-month commitments,* which becomes a poor choice to advertise a **time-sensitive** announcement.

Once a billboard is seen over and over again, it is no longer just forgotten, it can become an **eye sore.**

Repetition only works when there is a message to remember. *Not just a street address.*

As Ted Sann, chairman-chief creative officer of Omnicom's BBDO Worldwide in New York once said:

"If the ad is recalled but not liked, what's the point?"

Instead of creating immovable messages for moving targets, reset your budgets for where the two meet: *at the movies.*

PUSH

A center of *attention* can also
be a center of *distraction*.

PIT
ITS

There's only one thing that
can trump purpose:

Position.

149

Palm Sunday

Long story short, I wasn't the biggest palm waver growing up.

I always wondered as a child why the *same people* waving palms on that great and triumphant day, were some of the *same people* screaming **'Crucify Him'** just a few days later.

I'm quite sure that donkey ride into Jerusalem had to be incredible to witness firsthand. But watching those *palm wavers* turn on a dime was probably a real sight to see too.

From **'Hosanna'** to **'Barabbas'** - not sure there has ever been a larger demonstration of public *betrayal*.

Love Offering

When in doubt, keep your pastor **on salary.**
His service is NOT voluntary, so neither should his *reward* be.

If you're not careful, love offerings can easily
become gratuitous if constantly asked for.

Besides, no congregation is immune to **head counters.**
They're everywhere.

Let's not hinge our pastors' house payments on them.
Not wise at all.

The
Marketing
Department

I love marketing.
Correction: I heart *GREAT* marketing.

So much so, that I've sort of become 'that marketing guy' within my own small circle of peers and friends.

So I'm sure this one will come as a bit of a surprise to many. I'll never forget this quote I once read from marketing guru **Seth Godin*** as it relates to the down side of his profession:

*"In my experience, much of marketing is a game of waiting for the other guy to **go first.**"*

While the 'other guy' Seth was referring to in this case was the leading competitor of any particular company or organization, when it comes to the growing number of marketing departments that exist within today's churches…

…the other guy has (unfortunately) become the pastor.

Most church marketing departments are designed to simply **ADVERTISE** a product / or service their pastor desires to sell...

...rather than to assist in the actual **CREATION** and **IMPLEMENTATION** of that product or service.

Big difference there.

If you're not going to allow your marketing department to be involved with your product on the *front side,* then maybe it's time you get rid of them altogether until you're ready to do so.

If you insist on keeping it, then I highly recommend changing the name from the **MARKETING** department...

...to the **COMMUNICATIONS** department.

Doing so will begin fostering a *creative environment* where those 'marketing guys' can begin asking the right questions:

WHAT? WHY? *and* HOW?

Instead of just asking the wrong ones:

WHO? *and* WHEN?

*See page 86 for more with Seth Godin. As you can see, I'm a big fan.

Hope you will be too.

Church Vans

Get rid of our church vans?
Give me one good reason why we should?

OK. I'll give you **432.**

Ever since 1982, when the 15-passenger vans burst
onto the scene, there have been more than
432 fatalities due to *van rollovers.*

Need another number? Let's try **881.**

That's the number of **incapacitating injuries** that
have been reported from van rollovers.

So why the high rollover rate?

Simply because 15-passenger vans were unfortunately created to have a high center of gravity.

The center shifts higher and rearward the **more** people board a van.

Braking suddenly or making slight turns can cause major stability problems for these vans, despite a driver's experience.

Without dual rear wheels, which very few are built with, these vans are **extremely dangerous** on the road.

Not exactly the kind of vehicles you want your precious youth group to be riding in.

So what's the solution?
Purchase 15 passenger **BUSES.**

They come with dual rear wheels.
Center aisles.
Rear emergency doors.

And best of all, a CDL license is not required to drive one.

Sure, they may cost a few extra bucks, but there are some things in life you just can't put a price tag on.

Safety is one of them.

(shout out to the late Marvin Brown, the finest church bus driver the world has ever known. As you can see, I was listening.)

Announcement Reading

Don't just read one.

CREATE ONE!

If what you're announcing is not *a hoax*,
then please, by all means...

...GO ALL OUT!

Audio Cassette
& VHS Tape Product Sales

Shouldn't have to say much about this.

But for those of you out there **still selling** these in your church bookstore, hoping they'll one day make a comeback…

…trust me. It's not going to happen.

Besides, basic DVDs will almost become extinct in about a year or two. **Blue-Ray** now has a permanent seat at the table.

New Rule: Sell CDs and DVDs on-site at your church only.

But when off-site and online, sell downloadable(s) only. Try to save on shipping and packaging whenever you can.

What's that you say?

"What about the people who don't have a computer?"

Funny you would ask that.

Anyone remember Blockbuster Video?

They held on to that same old sale pattern so long,
they became irrelevant.

Hello Netflix.
And now, hello Hulu.

Volunteer Church Security Guard

Sept. 16, 1999: Seven young people were killed when a man opened fire during a prayer service for teen-agers at the Wedgewood Baptist Church in Fort Worth, Texas.

Oct. 5, 2003: A woman opened fire in Turner Monumental AME church in Kirkwood, east of Atlanta, killing the pastor and two others.

March 12, 2005: A man walked into the services of the Living Church of God in Milwaukee and open fired immediately, killing seven people.

April 9, 2005: A 27-year-old airman died after being shot at a church in College Park, Ga., where he had once worked as a security guard.

Feb. 26, 2006: Two people were killed at Zion Hope Missionary Baptist Church in Michigan by a man who reportedly went to the church looking for his girlfriend.

May 21, 2006: Four were killed by a man at Jesus Christ Church in Louisiana.

Oct. 2, 2006: Although not at a church building, an attack in Lancaster County, Pa., by a gunman who killed five girls and then himself at an Amish school, targeted a religious site.

May 20, 2007: A standoff between police and a suspect in the shootings of three people in a Moscow, Idaho, Presbyterian Church ended with three dead, including one police officer.

August 12, 2007: A lone gunman, Eiken Elam Saimon, opened fire in a Missouri Micronesian church, killing a pastor and two other churchgoers.

Dec. 9, 2007: Gunman shoots and kills four people in a shooting spree at a megachurch in Colorado Springs and a missionary training school near Denver.

July 27, 2008: Lone gunman shoots and kills two people at the Tennessee Valley Unitarian Universalist Church.

March 8, 2009: Gunman shoots and kills pastor at First Baptist Maryville (Illinois), and wounds several others with knife.

August 23, 2009: Oklahoma pastor Carol Daniels is slain in her church with multiple stab wounds to the neck and chest.

If security at your church is still on a **volunteer basis,** maybe its time you consider upgrading.

You can't put a cap on crazy these days.

The Benevolence Fund

Let's just be honest for a second here.

The line is always a mile long for people who believe
that churches today don't give enough to those in need.

However, I think it's time I start a **new line.**

One for people (like me) who believe that some of
our churches today...may be giving away *too much*.

I realize the statement above may sound a bit ridiculous,
but after reading this, you may just change your mind.

At least I hope so; I'd hate to be in this line all by myself.

In Acts 3, two of Christ's disciples-soon-to-be-apostles,
Peter and John, were on their way to a temple to pray.

As they approached the temple's gate, they saw a lame man
lying in front, asking all who were entering the temple for help.

Not just any kind of help.

But the kind of help most people all over the world ask
for every single day: **Financial help.**

So just as he had done with everyone else on that day,
the lame man proceeded to ask Peter and John for help as well.

And it is here where the story gets interesting.

In verse 4 of the chapter, the writer says that Peter, standing beside John, 'fixed' his eyes on the lame man.

Another translation says that Peter 'fastened' his eyes upon him.

I found it interesting that the word 'fasten' in the Greek literally means "to look **INTO** or to fix one's mind on someone as an **EXAMPLE**."

So with eyes now looking onto (and into) the lame man, Peter, one never known to mince his words, then said, *"Look at us."*

I have to admit, I just love this passage of scripture.

For hidden within it lies an **exchange of the heart** that many within our churches today tend to overlook when giving to those who are less fortunate.

From the AIDS infected villages of Uganda, to the homeless tent cities now emerging in Sacramento, California, there is literally no corner of the world you and I can travel to where we will not encounter those who are in need.

As our nation's economy continues to struggle, our churches are often *overwhelmed* with an increasing amount of people who find themselves physically and financially lame and with a pure and sincere heart, looking for some kind of assistance.

Yet, here in this passage, Peter and John do something **very few** churches do.

They looked "into" the lame man.
In other words, they made an assessment.

An assessment of not only what the man was truly in need of,
but also (as we read later on) an assessment of what they were
capable of providing, which as it turns out, was not alms at all.

But faith.

It is unfortunate how so many of our churches today have often
taken on the incredible burden of healing the many, without taking
the time necessary to properly assess the *'one.'*

What is the **ONE** need our church has been placed here
(within this community) to heal?

What is the **ONE** problem our church has been best designed
and empowered by God with the necessary resources to fix?

If we as believers, as well as the respective churches we attend,
can ever take the time out to properly identify what that **ONE**
need and problem God has for us to address, the chances of it
no longer being a problem will increase exponentially.

Nothing tears at my heart more than to see a homeless man sitting
at a nearby intersection in need of food, and after giving him the
few dollars I have on me to give, find him sitting there again at
that same intersection the following week.

Still in need.
Still in hunger

Our approach to giving must become **more strategic** if we are ever going to make a lasting difference in the earth today.

I have always been amazed at how Christ would often find Himself in the middle of a crowd, a crowd of lame, sick, and hurting people, and instead of healing the entire crowd...

...He would choose to only heal one.

Isn't it interesting that this same lame man was laid daily at the **very gate** that Christ himself, before ever being crucified, would pass in order to enter the temple to pray and teach? (See John 7:14; John 10:23)

With a ministry that only spanned a total of 3 years, it is quite possible that Christ saw this lame man during one of his visits to the temple, but decided to **heal another**, instead of him.

Perhaps in God's providential plan, Christ **passed over** the opportunity to heal this man, knowing that the day would come when Peter and John would return to that same temple gate and provide us all with (what I believe) is one of the best *benevolence* and *giving strategies* ever created:

ASSESS what you have.
GIVE what you can.

But when you cannot give,
REFER UP or **MOBILIZE.**

"Silver and gold I do not have, but what I do have I give you: In the name of Jesus Christ of Nazareth, rise up and walk" - Acts 3:6

167

The Ministry Acronym

I'm not sure when it happened.

But the **MINISTRY ACRONYM** has passed away.
Cause of death remains unknown.

I do have one theory: *over usage.*

In an age where so much ingenuity is available to the church through its **younger members**, it's amazing the acronym still can't find any peace.

Please. Stop using acronyms for our ministry programs or events.

We can squeeze the very life and creativity out of a new **OUTREACH** project if we insist on telling people it will:

Outwardly.

Unify.

The.

Redeemed.

Even.

As.

Christ.

Has.

Besides being a tad bit corny, we can force someone to have an aneurysm trying to search for words in order to *sound spiritual.*

168

Deacon-Led Worship

Likewise, deacons must be reverent, not double-tongued,
not given to much wine, not greedy for money,
holding the mystery of the faith with a pure conscience.
- 1 Timothy 3:8-9

Maybe that's the **mystery** Paul was talking about all along.

One would have to admit that for a deacon to insist
on singing Sunday after Sunday completely
out of tune truly takes a *pure conscience.*

It's obvious he just doesn't know.

the
USHER
board

Isn't it amazing what we can find in *the dark*
(i.e., a movie theater), we can't find in *the light*.

There is a huge difference between ushering people
INTO a building, and ushering people **WITHIN** it.

It is no secret among my friends and family members that
one of my favorite places in the world is **Best Buy;**
especially on Tuesdays, when new DVD releases hit the shelf.

In my opinion, there is no church in America that has a
better **usher board** then Best Buy.

They have mastered the art of hosting their guests
better than anyone I have ever seen.

As you walk into their store, you will be greeted by one of their employees, who is paid to stay in **one place** the entire day.

Right by the door.

He or she will welcome you, and when you're finished shopping with them, they will greet you as you leave.

From the same spot.

Creating opportunities for your guests to walk around and discover what they're looking for is a great way of ensuring your guests will return again.

Nothing can be worse than an usher who insists on filling up an empty seat in the middle of the pew, despite the fact that it would require someone *crossing the legs* of at least 11 people to do so.

The last pair of legs belonging to someone who was just about to pray to God for the **first time** in over a month.

Or that usher who just loves to escort all of the young college students to *the front* of the church, many of whom are still wearing what they had on at the club the night before.

Your approach to ushering people **IN**, may become the same approach that will usher people right **OUT** of your church.

Never to come back.

Better to leave some seats **empty** this Sunday than to have a difficulty filling them up next Sunday.

And now, believe it or not, this is the **MOST IMPORTANT** reason why I wrote this book. The first *82 things* were just to warm you up.

172

The "Black Church" Phrase

In May of 2008, I picked up a copy of a well-known local newspaper and was rather shocked, but overcome with excitement to see the front page headline read:

"Morehouse (College) Valedictorian Stands Out; He's White!"

Morehouse College, the only all-male **historically black** institution of higher learning in the United States, made history that year by announcing that the valedictorian of the graduating class of 2008, was a 22-year old **white male** from Kansas City, Missouri.

Now before I go any further, allow me to pause here just for a second, and take a deep breath.

{sigh}

For what you are about to read now may in fact be the hardest thing I have ever had to write.

I pray it serves as just one small verse in the anthem God seems to be birthing within the hearts of many within my generation who are as in love with the local church as I am.

What began as a badge of honor has now become
(in my opinion) one of the **largest hindrances** for growth
and our ability to impact today's emerging culture and society.

There is little doubt in my mind that during the height of slavery and
Jim Crow, it was not only wise, but in many instances, **a matter of law**
for Sunday morning to be the most *segregated* hour in America.

The civic and religious discrimination that African-Americans faced
particularly during the 1800's, provided the necessary backdrop for
many to be led, and at times, forced to create and provide
new outlets of worship that spoke specifically to the needs and
concerns of African-Americans.

Sidenote: Although I use the term 'African-American' here,
I realize a few other labels were used during those times as well
(i.e., colored, black, negro, etc.).

Just figured I would choose one for now.

No one can argue that the **'black church'** was at the very core of what
helped shape the cultural landscape of this country:

The civil rights movement.

Who can possibly deny its influence?

America is in many respects what the **'black church'**
helped influenced it to be.

Well, now that I've got all that out the way...

...ladies and gentlemen, this is 2010.
I repeat; the year is 2010.

Now before you assume I am saying that racism and discrimination is now over, that is **NOT** at all what I'm saying.

I do NOT, like so many of my peers, believe we are living in a *post-racial* America now that our country has elected its first African-American president.

Issues of race (in my opinion) are here to stay.

What I am saying is that the scope of the church, specifically the **'black church,'** must begin to change.

For many, it has.
Yet for a large majority, it has not.

I have tossed this question around in my head for about a year now. Haven't settled on the answer yet, although I think I'm pretty close.

Maybe you can help me.

It's one of those which-came-first (the chicken or the egg) type of questions. Here it is:

What comes first:
The 'local' church or the 'black' church?

I realize that may be a loaded question, but I'm curious how in this day and age, when so many of what we call **'black churches'** are no longer only located in urban or predominately African-American neighborhoods, but also in suburban and relatively multi-cultural communities...

...how is that we can still (with a clear conscience) label our churches as **'black?'**

For the record: I, too, am a proud graduate of an historically black college. Yet one of the things I admire most is that it was just that:

An **'historically'** black college.

Yes, the college was 'historically' founded exclusively for African-American

But my education, although some job recruiters would love to think so, was not framed by color alone.

It was framed by mission.

Had my education simply been framed by color, I would not have been able to compete in a world that color still may influence, but no longer dominates.

My fear with the continuous usage of the phrase **'the black church,'** is that it often haphazardly places a label on mission, and not solely on the predominate ethnic makeup of one's congregation.

Which leaves this question to consider:
What do you do when the ethnic makeup changes?

Are you still a **'black church'** when Hispanic believers and non- believers choose to attend?

Are you still a **'black church'** when Caucasian or Asian believers and non-believers attend?

How is it that we can allow color predominance to dictate what the *mission* and *focus* of the local church should be?

I might be a little crazy in saying this, but I think these labels are now killing the heart of what the **'black church'** actually once represented:

Compassion.
Change.
Resistance.

And most imporantly,

Movement.

I think in many respects, the success we achieved during the civil rights era of the 1950's and '60's has caused an entire new generation of leaders to misinterpret what the local church was really all about.

We must understand that for many of us now, we eat from vineyards we **did not plant.**

And because we did not work for what we are eating, many of us have ceased from working at all.

Our buildings are magnificent, but our scope of care has not grown to touch the lives of those who do not look like us.

There is a major difference between pride and **self-segregation.**

And many of us are beginning to be anchored in the latter.

Although this shift will take some time and a whole lot of effort, we must come to an agreement that what began with us, must **no longer** (only) be about us.

We can no longer afford to call or describe our places of worship as a **'black church.'**

That is one phrase (I believe) we must get rid of,
and we must do so immediately.

For if we don't, we will give birth yet again to a generation of believers
who have no problem acknowledging their **MOTHER**, but continue to
have no authentic and substantial relationship with their **FATHER.**

*"In this manner, therefore, pray: Our Father in heaven,
Hallowed be Your name…" – Matthew 6:9*

Our roots must extend **further** than Mother Africa.

For beyond that land lies a kingdom established by a **Father**
who loves us, and sent His Son to die for us all.

God I pray we never become more **BLACK,**
than we are **CHRISTIAN.**

thanks for reading.

now, i dare you to do one of the following two things:

1. Share and discuss this book with **someone else.**
(i guarantee you the conversations will
be nothing short of incredible.)

and...

2. Log onto **http://83thingsbook.com** and leave a
comment or two about this book. I'd love to hear from you!

meet milan

Milan Ford has been a leader and *survivor* of ministry within the local church for most of his life.

A lover of Red Vines Licorice and all things pointing North, Milan currently serves as a content editor and marketing director for a number of online Christian networks.

A full-time graduate student, Milan now consults a number of churches in areas of student ministry, marketing, online campus strategies, and leadership...

...while in preparation for something involving *a path, and a bridge*.

Milan and his wife *Imani* are the proud parents of three children: *Kayla, Aliyah, and Ethan*.

You can either follow him at **twitter.com/milanford** or find him rambling and writing at **ThePewView.com.**

You can also find him at **facebook.com/milanford.** But not too often *(he's trying to cut back).*

acknowledgements

I would like to thank my wife *Imani*, and my three children, *Kayla, Aliyah, and Ethan* for finding the room in their hearts to love the back of my head while I sat at my computer night after night to write this book.

My face is always yours.

To Lisa Birch, the best kept secret in the ATL.

To Jason Benjamin, for framing this book beautifully in less than 70 seconds.

To Tanya James, for making my life easier.

To Seth Godin, Renewed Vision and PJ Morton, for saying 'YES'.

And to my friends *Leigh Germy, AM Design,* and *Power Publishing Inc.* - we'll meet again!

I would also like to thank the countless numbers of *friends, followers, and fans* who helped to keep me in between the walls of **offense** and **relevance** while writing this book.

I could not have struck this balance without you.

And lastly, to *Elder Pat Riley,* who back in 2007, in front of a packed church audience one Sunday morning, gave me the greatest compliment I've ever received in my life.

"I'm so glad Milan is on our side."

a path and a bridge

I am often asked why i call myself a ministry **'survivor.'**
Well, sometime next fall (2010), I plan to tell the world why.

Stay tuned; another book is underway.

LaVergne, TN USA
03 November 2010

203372LV00007B/143/P